I0605345

FRACTURED AMERICA

The Damage Caused by False Information and Conspiracy Theories

John Allen

San Diego, CA

About the Author
John Allen is a writer who lives in Oklahoma City.

Printed in the United States

For more information, contact:
ReferencePoint Press, Inc.
PO Box 27779
San Diego, CA 92198
www.ReferencePointPress.com

LIBRARY OF CONGRESS CATALOGING-IN-PUBLICATION DATA

Names: Allen, John, 1957- author
Title: Fractured America : the damage caused by false information and conspiracy theories / by John Allen.
Description: San Diego, CA : ReferencePoint Press, Inc, 2026. | Includes bibliographical references and index.
Identifiers: LCCN 2025030928 (print) | LCCN 2025030929 (ebook) | ISBN 9781678210823 library binding | ISBN 9781678210830 ebook
Subjects: LCSH: Misinformation--United States--Juvenile literature | Disinformation--United States--Juvenile literature | Conspiracy theories--United States--Juvenile literature
Classification: LCC HM1231 .A55 2026 (print) | LCC HM1231 (ebook)
LC record available at https://lccn.loc.gov/2025030928
LC ebook record available at https://lccn.loc.gov/2025030929

CONTENTS

Trading in False Information

In March 2025 Joe Rogan, America's number one podcaster on Spotify, interviewed Darryl Cooper, a self-styled historian of World War II. Cooper took the opportunity to air his outrageous views on Nazi Germany and the Holocaust. He defended his claim that Nazi leader Adolf Hitler had sincerely wanted peace not war. He claimed that Nazi death camps were not intended for killing Jews but were originally built to deal humanely with a flood of prisoners of war. During the interview, Rogan did offer his own pushback—not against Cooper, but against those who call him an apologist for Nazi Germany. Rogan suggested that Jews who condemned Cooper's views were paranoid and prone to overreaction.

Other podcasters with wide followings, such as Tucker Carlson, have also hosted Cooper and given his ideas serious attention. Carlson called Cooper "the best and most honest popular historian in the United States."[1] Critics of these podcasters see their trade in false information as a dangerous sign. "Tens of millions of people will hear this grimy sociohistorical discourse," says Abe Greenwald in a newsletter for *Commentary*. "How many of them will disagree with it? Even if it's a majority—*if*—that leaves millions who will accept it at face value."[2]

Misinformation and Hatred Giving Rise to Violence

False information such as the historical lies spread by Cooper and other so-called historians can lead to all sorts of bad consequences. Radical right-wing groups and neo-Nazis use such falsehoods to support their own violent rhetoric. They also push long-debunked conspiracy theories, such as claims about secret Jewish control of global finance. Adding to the anti-Semitic climate in America are recent attacks on Jewish students by left-wing campus groups at major universities, including Columbia and Harvard. In April 2025 an in-house investigative report at Harvard revealed a pattern of harassment and threats against Jewish students at the university.

Watchdog groups document how misinformation and hatred can give rise to violence. In October 2024 the Anti-Defamation League reported a historic spike in threats and attacks against Jews in America over the previous year. The organization compiled a list of more than ten thousand anti-Semitic incidents during that period, an increase of 360 percent. Of these incidents, 634 were attacks and threats of violence on synagogues and Jewish community centers.

A History of Conspiracy Theories and Violence

False information, conspiracy theories, and political violence have a long history in America. The November 1963 assassination of President John F. Kennedy spawned a seemingly endless stream of books and documentaries claiming that Kennedy's murder was the result of a conspiracy. The September 11, 2001, terrorist attacks on the World Trade Center in New York City and the Pentagon in Washington, DC, also has sparked repeated conspiracy theories. Mere hours after the attacks, posts appeared online blaming the attacks not on the terrorist group al Qaeda but on the US government or Israel. Shadowy right-wing groups such as QAnon claim that a so-called deep state, made up of covert officials inside the federal government, was responsible for the attacks. Such theories continue to affect public opinion. More than two decades after the events, a significant number of Americans still question the official account.

On January 6, 2021, then-president Donald Trump's false claims of widespread voting fraud and stolen votes led some of his followers to storm the US Capitol.

Today's deep divide over politics in America has created an atmosphere in which disputes about elections and vote counts have the potential for violence. On January 6, 2021, then-president Donald Trump's false claims of widespread voting fraud and stolen votes led some of his followers to storm the US Capitol. They tried, without success, to stop Congress's certification of the presidential election results. In the melee that followed, one protester was killed and 138 Capitol Police and Metropolitan Police officers were injured, some severely.

The Threat of Misinformation to Public Health

Misinformation and conspiracy theories have increasingly become staples on social media and extremist websites. They not only sow confusion but also can present a serious threat to pub lic health. An outbreak of measles in West Texas in late January 2025 was blamed on parents who refused to let their children be vaccinated. Their refusal was based on false reports that the vaccine for measles could lead to autism and other health problems for recipients. Lower vaccination rates enabled the measles outbreak to spread to other states. At least three children died from a disease that had been all but eradicated in recent years. Potentially adding to the problem, Trump's choice for his administration's director of the US Department of Health and Human Services was Robert F. Kennedy Jr., a longtime vaccine skeptic.

> **"Whether we like it or not, social media is the public square of the 21st century. If we allow it to devolve into a battlefield of unchecked vitriol and deception, first the most vulnerable among us will pay the price, and then we all will."[3]**
>
> —Fay M. Johnson, former trust and safety product executive at Meta, Twitter (now X), and Nextdoor

The spread of false information about so many key issues, from elections to vaccines, has created a growing climate of distrust in America. Debates have arisen on how to balance free speech rights with the need to curb sources of misinformation. "Whether we like it or not, social media is the public square of the 21st century," says Fay M. Johnson, former trust and safety product executive at Meta, Twitter (now X), and Nextdoor. "If we allow it to devolve into a battlefield of unchecked vitriol and deception, first the most vulnerable among us will pay the price, and then we all will."[3]

CHAPTER ONE

How Misinformation and Conspiracy Theories Spread

When several large wildfires broke out in the Los Angeles area in January 2025, social media sites became filled with startling images of the destruction. Some video clips were offered as proof that the fires were deliberately ignited by a military laser weapon or microwave system. One clip showed the famous Hollywood sign engulfed in flames. An aerial video focused on a red-roofed building, supposedly a mosque, that remained untouched by the fire while all the structures around it burned. Panic about riots and looting arose in response to videos that showed thieves emptying out houses in the path of the flames. Many online observers rushed to share these videos with friends or followers.

There was a problem, however—the videos were either falsified images or taken out of context. The flame-engulfed Hollywood sign was a deepfake video, which anyone could have discovered by checking Google or the sign's own website. The video of the mysteriously untouched building with the red roof did not show the Los Angeles blazes. It was shot during the wildfires on the Hawaiian island of Maui in August 2023. And the footage that claimed to depict looting actually showed friends and workers removing items from houses in the path of the Los Angeles inferno. Experts have often debunked claims that laser or microwave weapons have ever been used to ignite wildfires. Yet certain conspiracy-minded individuals continue to spread these false stories and fake videos. Such people need to find a scapegoat for disasters that seem dangerously out of control. "People blame the government or company executives because it's easier than facing structural problems, like drought conditions," says Geoff Dancy, a political science professor at the University of Toronto. "That is more attractive to people that are desperate for order amid catastrophe."[4]

Erosion of Faith in America's Institutions

The growth of misinformation and conspiracy theories has played a large part in creating today's political and social divisions in the United States. Worst of all is disinformation, or deliberate attempts to mislead people or spread propaganda. The sheer volume of falsehoods and distortions of the truth threaten to erode people's faith in American institutions, including democracy. A July 10, 2024, survey by the Pew Research Center found that 72 percent

After the 2025 Los Angeles fires broke out, as pictured here, many social media sites contained images of the fires that were falsified or taken out of context.

of Americans no longer believe that the United States is a good example of democracy. Another 8 percent maintain that it has never been a good example for other countries to follow.

Americans also consider misinformation to be a significant threat to society. A November 2023 survey conducted by the School of Thought International, a nonprofit that studies critical thinking, found that 84 percent of Americans worry about the impact of misinformation. Seventy-eight percent see it as an existential threat to American society. The survey also discovered that people trust family members and friends more than traditional news sources such as CNN, *The New York Times*, and Fox News. "Many are concerned about misinformation and disinformation but don't know what to do about it," says Sander van der Linden, a Cambridge University professor who led the survey. "We're advocating for governments, organizations, and people around the world to join us in taking an evidence-based approach to address this problem and work together to mitigate its effects."[5] One bright spot van der Linden and his colleagues found was that a majority of respondents saw the need to develop critical thinking skills, including the ability to spot fake news and propaganda.

"Many are concerned about misinformation and disinformation but don't know what to do about it. We're advocating for governments, organizations, and people around the world to join us in taking an evidence-based approach to address this problem."[5]

—Sander van der Linden, professor at Cambridge University

Misinformation and disinformation can also affect citizens' ability to cast informed votes. False claims about candidates or their policies can leave voters confused and even convince them to vote against their own best interests. Personal attacks on candidates based on lies and exaggerations tend to increase voter hostility and feed into extremism. Fake stories about rigged elections and security problems with voting machines, vote counts, and mail-in votes lead people to distrust the whole election system. Too often the true story gets less attention than the scandalous lie. "Truth is boring, facts are boring, and outrage is really interesting," says Utah Lieutenant Governor Deidre Henderson, a Republican who supervises elections in her

Fake News That Spreads like a Virus

Virtually everyone has heard about stories or memes that go viral on the internet, meaning they spread rapidly across social media platforms in a short time. But experts on information sharing say that fake news really does spread like a highly contagious virus. Such viral content is quick to generate millions of likes, shares, views, and comments, often before efforts to debunk the stories can even begin. "Scientists have found a close analogy between the spread of misinformation and the spread of viruses," say British academics Sander van der Linden and David Robert Grimes, who have led surveys of social media use. "In fact, how misinformation gets around can be effectively described using mathematical models designed to simulate the spread of pathogens."

So if misinformation is like a human virus, then the solution is finding a way to counter its spread. Researchers have turned to an approach called psychological inoculation, or prebunking. This means introducing and then refuting common falsehoods about election fraud or other issues so that people gain immunity to certain kinds of fake news. "It's similar to vaccination," say Van der Linden and Grimes, "where people are introduced to a (weakened) dose of the virus to prime their immune systems to future exposure."

Sander van der Linden and David Robert Grimes, "Misinformation Really Does Spread like a Virus, Suggest Mathematical Models Drawn from Epidemiology," The Conversation, November 5, 2024. https://theconversation.com.

state. "It's like playing whack-a-mole with truth. But what we try to do is just get as much information out there as possible."[6]

A healthy democracy depends on the losing side accepting the results—and not launching wild conspiracy theories about voting fraud and stolen elections. Such reckless falsehoods, even when countered with facts, tend to sow doubts among potential voters. They can also lead to violence, as with the January 6 storming of the Capitol by Trump supporters. Repeated on message boards and in podcasts, these falsehoods inevitably have a corrosive effect. Recent polling by the Pew Research Center and others indicates that many people are starting to lose faith in democratic norms.

Tracking the Spread of Misinformation

The internet and social media make up the digital superhighway that allows misinformation and propaganda to flow almost unimpeded twenty-four hours a day. False information and deliberate disinformation can spread like a virus through social media sites like X, Bluesky, Facebook, Instagram, TikTok, and others. The popular phrase "going viral" indicates how rapidly information, both legitimate and bogus, can speed across the internet. Social media sites vary widely in their approach to policing misinformation. For example, Twitter used to prohibit spreading false or misleading information about topics such as election security or COVID-19 protocols. Following tech billionaire Elon Musk's October 2022 acquisition of the company, which he renamed X, these prohibitions were either scrapped or greatly eased. In September 2023, X announced it would no longer allow people to report posts on the site for being false or misleading. As Miah Hammond-Errey, director of the University of Sydney's Emerging Technology Program, wrote in the magazine *Foreign Policy*:

> Few recent actions have done more to make a social media platform safe for disinformation, extremism, and authoritarian regime propaganda than the changes to Twitter since its purchase by Elon Musk in 2022. Following his takeover as CEO [chief executive officer], the platform has disbanded its trust and safety teams; revoked bans on extremist and dangerous accounts; removed labels informing users that accounts were associated with foreign governments (including Russian and Chinese propaganda outlets); censored journalists critical of Musk; and allowed for what users report, anecdotally, to be a sharp increase in hate speech, online trolling, and harassment. All this marks the decline of Twitter as a trusted platform for news and information.[7]

In January 2025 the social networking giant Meta announced that it was discontinuing its use of third-party fact-checkers on Facebook, Instagram, and Threads. Previously, outside fact-checking groups could flag posts that allegedly contained misinformation, disinformation, or hate speech. Serious abuses could lead to users being banned from a platform. However, under its new policy, Meta will rely on users to correct false or misleading

After Twitter became X, prohibitions on spreading false or misleading information were scrapped or greatly eased.

content. Tech watchdog companies immediately condemned Meta's decision. Mark Zuckerberg, chair and CEO of Meta, was widely viewed as bowing to pressure from the incoming Trump administration in making the change. "Let's be clear: Meta's decision to end fact-checking is a gift to Donald Trump and extremists around the world," says Nicole Gill, cofounder and executive director of Accountable Tech. "Now, Zuckerberg is re-opening the floodgates to the exact same surge of hate, disinformation, and conspiracy theories that caused January 6th—and that continue to spur real-world violence. . . . The world will be far more dangerous as a result."[8]

Misinformation also arises on message board sites such as Reddit and Quora, where people go to engage in lively exchanges of ideas and opinions. Discussions on Reddit threads are preserved in archives, usually after six months, meaning new comments and upvotes or downvotes are no longer accepted. Moderators can turn the archiving feature on or off for their

> **"Let's be clear: Meta's decision to end fact-checking is a gift to Donald Trump and extremists around the world. . . . The world will be far more dangerous as a result."[8]**
>
> —Nicole Gill, cofounder and executive director of Accountable Tech

own threads. Nonetheless, archived posts remain visible and open to user searches for years. The archives enable false information and propaganda to reach new readers long after the original conversation has ended. Reddit users have no way to correct misinformation or clarify what was posted.

Old material on websites is preserved on the Internet Archive, a nonprofit digital library, and less extensive versions such as Pagefreezer, Stillio, and Archive.today. The Internet Archive's Wayback Machine bills itself as a history of humanity online, with more than 900 billion web pages in its online library. But these archives focus on preservation, not correction. Therefore, they do not generally engage in fact-checking or editing of content. This means that past examples of false or misleading information remain available for potential misuse.

Spreading Misinformation via Technology

Technology offers lots of ways to amplify misinformation and conspiracy theories. Bots (short for *robots*) are software programs that imitate human activities, such as communication. These automated social media accounts are programmed to share online content and interact with other users. Their ability to flood social media sites with misinformation and manipulate online debates makes them a dangerous component on social media. With artificial intelligence (AI) advances, bots can be difficult to detect, even during online exchanges. Telltale signs can include accounts whose responses are extremely rapid, accounts whose posts or likes appear at an unnatural rate, or similar accounts that share the same content repeatedly.

Russia has used bots to influence the last three American elections and spread lies on many other issues. In July 2024 the US Department of Justice, working with partners in Canada and Netherlands, broke up a Russian bot farm that was spreading pro-Russian propaganda about the war in Ukraine. AI enabled these bots to create a message, adapt it to different audiences, and distribute it instantly. Russian bots are also employed

Using Deepfakes to Spread Disinformation

A somber video of Ukrainian president Volodymyr Zelenskyy shows him announcing his nation's surrender to Russia. Blurry photographs depict then–presidential candidate Donald Trump fighting police as they attempt to arrest him. A news video presents an English-speaking female anchor praising China for its leading role as peacemaker in an international summit. These items vary in quality of presentation. For example, Zelenskyy's head seems to be perched on an unusually long neck. But all of them share one attribute: They are so-called deepfakes, designed to fool unwary viewers.

In today's visual-oriented world, false or misleading photos and videos can often spread disinformation more effectively than text. Deepfake technology's potential to fool people has greatly increased with the advent of generative AI. Chatbots like ChatGPT enable deepfakes to mimic a person's gestures and voice with startling accuracy. Even deepfakes supposedly intended as jokes, like the Trump photos created by British journalist Eliot Higgins, can create confusion when shared online.

Tech experts have suggested ways to flag deepfakes by requiring them to have identifying watermarks or labels for safety. But rogue creators will be difficult to stop. According to Jack Stubbs, vice president at disinformation research firm Graphika, "What we're seeing today is another sign of things to come."

Quoted in Adam Satariano and Paul Mozur, "The People Onscreen Are Fake. The Disinformation Is Real," *New York Times*, February 27, 2023. www.nytimes.com.

to launch conspiracy theories that sow confusion and distrust among voters. According to Emily Harding, a director at the Center for Strategic and International Studies, "Russia has officially made one dystopian prediction about artificial intelligence (AI) come true: it used AI to lie better, faster, and more believably."[9]

Algorithms, or computerized rules and instructions, are another way technology contributes to the spread of misinformation and disinformation on social media sites. Algorithms are designed to deliver content to users based on metrics such as likes, shares, and comments. Thus, most content that users receive matches what they have seen before. This creates an echo chamber effect or feedback loop, in which users continually view content that confirms their prior beliefs. If what they believe is based on false

> **"Russia has officially made one dystopian prediction about artificial intelligence (AI) come true: it used AI to lie better, faster, and more believably."[9]**
>
> —Emily Harding, director at the Center for Strategic and International Studies

information or propaganda, algorithms help reinforce that deception by ensuring they receive more of the same. Algorithms also tend to emphasize content that is most likely to provoke strong emotions, such as fear, anger, or outrage. This can prompt users to share misinformation with others purely on impulse. Overall, say experts, the use of algorithms on social media has a polarizing influence and leads to extremism.

Anonymous Threats from the Dark Corners of the Internet

Some of the most extreme far-right political content online proceeds from imageboard sites like 4chan, 8kun, and a Russian version known as Dvach. The sites are called imageboards because each post begins with an image, such as a photo or cartoon. These dark corners of the internet, with their "anything goes" approach, enable users to post memes, text, and images anonymously. Not surprisingly, disinformation, hate speech, and conspiracy theories thrive in such an environment. In May 2019, 4chan gained notoriety for hosting a live stream of a terrorist attack on two mosques in Christchurch, New Zealand, in which fifty-one Muslims were killed. Through the years, the 4chan imageboard has purveyed wild conspiracy theories and threats of violence. In April 2025, 4chan fell prey to a suspected hack that left its future in question. The breach exposed internet protocol addresses linked to the site's users, which threatened to undermine their anonymity. "4chan is an anonymous message board that enables often offensive and hateful content," says Ian Gray, director of analysis and research at the security firm Flashpoint. "The content leaked, if genuine, would remove some of the anonymity from 4chan administrators, moderators, and janitors. Some users may have registered their email addresses years ago when they were less aware or concerned about their operational security."[10]

Whether on widely used social media sites or controversial imageboards like 4chan, misinformation and conspiracy theories

People mourn the victims of a terrorist attack on two mosques in Christchurch, New Zealand, in March 2019. A livestream of the attack was hosted by 4chan.

continue to spread online. Policies to fact-check and even remove false content have been moderated or scrapped altogether on many sites. Meanwhile, algorithms and AI technology tend to perpetuate misinformation on social media by constantly feeding users content that reinforces their opinions. Media experts and ordinary users alike warn that the rising tide of misinformation is only deepening the divisions in American society.

CHAPTER TWO

Elections and Conspiracy Theories

Two topics about which most Americans have strong opinions are elections and the weather. In October 2024, with a presidential election looming, these topics converged into a controversy. Many residents of western North Carolina were still reeling from the effects of Hurricane Helene, which had struck with devastating force in late September. Flooding, landslides, and blocked roads left large areas of Appalachia struggling to recover. As officials with the Federal Emergency Management Agency (FEMA) fanned out to offer assistance, conspiracy theories arose to question their efforts. A right-wing commentator named Jack Posobiec claimed that FEMA was engaging in voter suppression. He said FEMA agents were blocking relief and aid to prevent rural victims of Helene from voting in the upcoming election. Stories even circulated that the federal government had somehow manipulated the weather to target White, conservative voters.

Debunking Claims of Voter Suppression

Donald Trump, campaigning in the state for a second term as president, added to the confusion. He blasted FEMA for supposedly using up billions of disaster relief funds to help migrants who had entered the United States illegally. Trump's claim—like the other conspiracy theories, including the ones about voter suppression—was debunked by media sources and even by a Republican congressman traveling with him. However, the misinformation inflamed local opinion regarding FEMA and apparently led some people to threaten violence. At one point FEMA announced a temporary halt to rescue efforts when agents were harassed by an armed group in nearby Elk Mills, Tennessee. According to Carter County Sheriff Mike Fraley, no arrests were made, but the confrontation was tense. "It was a little hairy situation, no guns were drawn, but they were armed," Fraley told the Associated Press. "The community in that area has been great to work with, but this [armed] group is trying to create more hate toward the federal government."[11]

Several days after the election, some of the complaints about FEMA seemed to gain traction. The Daily Wire, a conservative media outlet, reported that FEMA agents in Lake Placid, Florida, working to help residents file for government aid after Hurricane Milton, were told via text messages to skip properties displaying Trump signs. "When we got there we were told to discriminate against people," a FEMA whistleblower told the outlet. "It's almost unbelievable to think that somebody in the federal government would think that's okay."[12] Soon thereafter FEMA fired the supervisor responsible for the messages.

With the American public so polarized politically, presidential elections are hotly contested and frequently decided by razor-thin margins. The outcome often depends on the so-called battleground states, or swing states, where a divided electorate makes every vote seem crucial. In such an atmosphere, people become more willing to believe that one side or the other is trying to gain an unfair advantage. Hot-button issues related to voting and vote counting, including mail-in voting, ballot harvesting, and use of voting machines, tend to attract even more scrutiny. Misinformation and conspiracy theories about election fraud find a willing audience, even as they undermine voters' faith in the integrity of the ballot.

False Claims of Election Fraud

Much of the misinformation about voter fraud and election rigging comes from Trump's false claims about the 2020 presidential election. Trump repeatedly insisted he had won the election, despite reviews and recounts that confirmed Joe Biden's victory.

Election analysts note that Biden's win was not especially close. He won by 306 votes to Trump's 232 in the Electoral College. His margin of victory in the popular vote was more than 7 million. The race was closer in the battleground states. But even there, most analyses show that Trump would have needed to flip more than 310,000 votes in six key states in order to win the election.

Nonetheless, Trump and his team responded to Biden's victory by repeating conspiracy theories about election fraud and filing numerous lawsuits. They falsely claimed that voting machines in certain states had switched votes from Trump to Biden. They contended that some states had counted more votes than their number of registered voters. But an exhaustive review of the election by the Associated Press in 2021 found fewer than 475 incidents of actual voter fraud across the six swing states, which was nowhere close to the totals needed to change the outcome. Dozens of courts, both state and federal, rejected Trump's legal challenges to the vote. US Circuit Judge Stephanos Bibas, serving on a federal panel that upheld Pennsylvania's results, expressed the judiciary's attitude toward Trump's lawsuits. "Voters, not lawyers, choose the president," said Bibas. "Ballots, not briefs, decide elections."[13] Moreover, secretaries of state around the nation, many of them Republicans, confirmed that the election had been safe and secure. Three weeks after the election, Trump's own attorney general, William Barr, declared that a US Department of Justice investigation had discovered no evidence of widespread voter fraud.

"Voters, not lawyers, choose the president. Ballots, not briefs, decide elections."[13]

—Stephanos Bibas, US circuit judge

Trump and his legal team's false allegations about voting machines also were debunked. The Cybersecurity and Infrastructure Security Agency, a US government agency that defends against cyber threats to American infrastructure, found no evidence that voting machines lost, deleted, or changed votes or were compromised in any way. That did not stop Trump's circle and personalities at Fox News from broadcasting the claims repeatedly. Dominion Voting Systems, which manufactured the machines in question, sued Fox

A Swatting Call to a Judge Presiding on Trump's Election Fraud Case

Late on a Sunday evening in January 2024, police in the District of Columbia responded to a call that reported a shooting at a residence. The home belonged to US District Judge Tanya Chutkan. The judge happened to be presiding over a criminal case that charged former president Trump with trying to overturn his defeat in the 2020 election. Trump had been appealing a ruling by Chutkan that denied his bid to dismiss the charges.

Police soon realized the call was a so-called swatting attempt. This involves a caller falsely reporting a crime in progress, which causes police to resort to emergency measures, often sending a SWAT team with weapons drawn. Swatting calls are intended to create anxiety for the subject and perhaps trigger a violent incident. Police reports in Chutkan's case revealed that no one was at home when the officers arrived.

Swatting incidents, often targeting election officials, are on the rise across the United States. Experts explain that the calls are an attempt to intimidate judges, government officials, and political opponents. As then–attorney general Merrick Garland said, "At the same time that we are seeing an encouraging downward trend in violent crime, we are also witnessing a deeply disturbing spike in threats against those who serve the public."

Quoted in Gabe Gutierrez et al., "Spate of Swatting Incidents Ensnares High-Profile Targets: Politicians, Prosecutors, and Judges," NBC News, January 10, 2024. www.nbcnews.com.

News for defamation. In April 2023, Fox News and its ownership group led by billionaire Rupert Murdoch, agreed to an out-of-court settlement in which they paid Dominion $787.5 million.

Trump's unsubstantiated claims about a stolen election ultimately led his supporters to storm the US Capitol on January 6, 2021, in a violent attack that shocked the nation. In February 2021 more questions about election integrity were raised from an unexpected source. In a cover story for *Time*, Molly Ball, a biographer of Speaker of the House Nancy Pelosi, described how Democrats, anti-Trump Republicans, and influential business titans had worked behind the scenes to ensure the election would be conducted securely. With COVID-19 restrictions in place, the conspirators acted to change election laws and rules to allow for more early voting and mail-in votes. According to Ball, they also wanted to avert the sort of street violence that had erupted in the protests over the death of George Floyd at the hands of police during the past summer. As Ball explained:

> That's why the participants want the secret history of the 2020 election told, even though it sounds like a paranoid fever dream—a well-funded cabal of powerful people, ranging across industries and ideologies, working together behind the scenes to influence perceptions, change rules and laws, steer media coverage and control the flow of information. They were not rigging the election; they were fortifying it.[14]

Between Trump's lies about a stolen election and Ball's assertion that a shadowy conspiracy was required to save democracy, Americans became even more divided along partisan lines regarding trust in the security and fairness of elections. A Gallup poll in November 2022 showed that 85 percent of Democrats and 67 percent of Independents had confidence in the accuracy of US elections, compared to only 40 percent of Republicans.

Bracing for a Resurgence of Falsehoods and Violence

In 2024 Americans braced themselves for a resurgence of misinformation and even possible violence in the run-up to the presidential election in November. In spite of attempts to keep Trump off the ballot in several states and his felony conviction in New York for falsifying business records, the former president easily won the Republican nomination. The campaign began as an expected rematch with Biden, who touted the fact that he had beaten Trump once and could do it again. But no one could have foreseen what quickly became the most chaotic presidential campaign in recent history.

On June 26 Biden faced off with Trump in a debate that was held unusually early in the campaign season. Before a national TV audience, the eighty-one-year-old Biden repeatedly stum

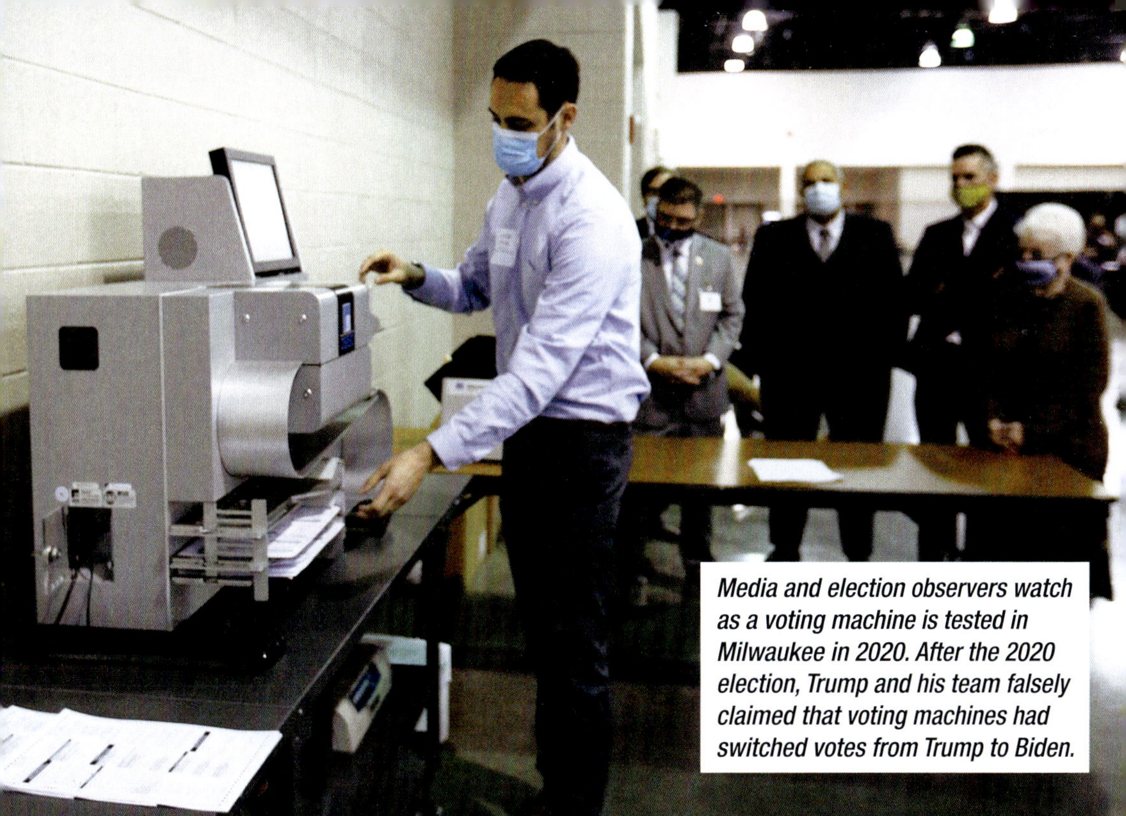

Media and election observers watch as a voting machine is tested in Milwaukee in 2020. After the 2020 election, Trump and his team falsely claimed that voting machines had switched votes from Trump to Biden.

bled over words, made unintelligible arguments, fumbled some of his prepared set-piece lines, and sometimes froze up entirely. His handlers initially blamed his disastrous performance on poor preparation, but the evidence of cognitive decline was impossible to ignore. A month later high-powered Democrats convinced Biden to step aside as candidate for the presidency in favor of his vice president, Kamala Harris.

Questions arose about how Biden's true cognitive state could have been hidden for so long by the White House inner circle. Critics also noted that many in the national media had dismissed evidence of Biden's decline and even attacked those who pointed it out. In May 2025, CNN news analyst Jake Tapper and Axios journalist Alex Thompson published *Original Sin: President Biden's Decline, Its Cover-Up, and His Disastrous Choice to Run Again* about the Biden situation. The book detailed how a conspiracy to cover up Biden's condition had led to electoral chaos.

After Biden dropped out, Trump raised public concerns surrounding the upcoming election by refusing to say whether he

Conspiracy Theories Persist After 2024 Election

The 2024 presidential election saw a different outcome from 2020, with former President Donald Trump winning a second term over Democrat Kamala Harris. The margin was decisive, though hardly the landslide victory that some Trump supporters claimed. Yet conspiracy theories about the outcome still arose on both political sides.

Some on the left claimed that Elon Musk's Starlink, a satellite-based internet provider, had been employed to change votes in Trump's favor. Right-wing conspiracy theorists, still obsessed with the 2020 result, insisted that 20 million fewer votes were cast in 2024, proving that Biden's total of 81 million votes had been bogus. Election monitors explained that the 20 million votes were not missing but were still being counted and Biden's total was correct. Nonetheless, the suspicions and accusations continued to fly. Election officials found the incessant false claims to be dispiriting as well as exhausting. As Gabriel Sterling, chief operating officer of the Georgia secretary of state's office, told CBS News, "Ideas that Musk's Starlink or black box voting might change votes plant seeds that will germinate into deeper conspiracy theories, and then further undermine faith in elections and institutions."

Quoted in David Becker, "Analysis: Election Conspiracies Persist, Even with Different Outcomes in the 2024 Election," CBS News, November 20, 2024. www.cbsnews.com.

would accept the result if he lost. The possibility of angry protests and mob violence, like the January 6 Capitol riot, served to keep much of the populace on edge throughout the campaign.

Debunking Election Misinformation and Conspiracy Theories

By October 2024 government leaders and election officials across the United States were working furiously to fend off a torrent of misinformation and conspiracy theories about the upcoming election. Right-wing sources insisted on the likelihood of election fraud and urged people to be on the lookout for irregularities. Stories spread about voting machines that could reverse votes by remote control; about how large numbers of noncitizens were likely to vote; about mail-in ballots that would be accepted without authentication or signatures; about supposed ballot harvesting schemes, in which ballots gathered in a neighborhood would be sifted to throw out the Trump votes; and about how districts in battleground states would tabulate more votes than the number of registered voters.

It became difficult for state election officials to keep up with all the fearmongering. However, they strived to debunk each false claim as it appeared. "It's reassuring how much better election officials have gotten around communication in advance of the election," said Bret Schafer, a senior fellow at the nonprofit Alliance for Securing Democracy. "There definitely wasn't the same level of interaction four years ago . . . in trying to communicate any changes in how voting will work this time, and, to the extent possible, short-circuit some of the false election narratives we know will be coming."[15]

"There definitely wasn't the same level of interaction four years ago . . . in trying to communicate any changes in how voting will work this time, and, to the extent possible, short-circuit some of the false election narratives we know will be coming."[15]

—Ben Schafer, senior fellow at Alliance for Securing Democracy

Several threatening incidents, some going back to early summer, had helped raise tensions preceding the election. In mid-June, an election office in Cuyahoga County, Ohio, had a third-floor window shattered by a gunshot. In September election offices and

An election worker removes ballots from a sorting machine in 2024. Security was increased at many polling locations in 2024.

secretaries of state in seventeen states received envelopes containing suspicious white powder. The return address on one envelope sent to Colorado Secretary of State Jena Griswold read "U.S. Traitor Elimination Army."[16] In October some election officials were the targets of false 911 calls about a bomb threat or active shooter. These ploys, called swatting, aim to have law enforcement officers arrive at a residence primed to deal with an emergency, often scaring victims or causing chaos. Faced with these threats and harassment, some election workers quit before the election.

To protect workers, many local election boards beefed up security at polling locations. Some polling places installed panic buttons keyed to a 911 dispatcher and erected bulletproof glass to protect against attacks. Tate Fall, election director for Cobb County, Georgia, says she became motivated to protect her poll workers after one of them was confronted during the March 2024 presidential primary by an agitated voter armed with a handgun. "That made it real for me—that it's so easy for something to go sideways in life, period, let alone the environment of Georgia and elections," says Fall. "I just can't have [poll workers] being harmed on my conscience."[17]

"It's so easy for something to go sideways in life, period, let alone the environment of Georgia and elections. I just can't have [poll workers] being harmed on my conscience."[17]

—Tate Fall, election director for Cobb County, Georgia

Polarization and closely contested elections in the United States have increased the spread of misinformation about voter fraud and rigged voting machines. Election officials have worked hard to debunk such claims, while also striving to protect election workers from outside threats. To preserve Americans' faith in democratic norms, officials continue to communicate the truth about US election integrity.

CHAPTER THREE

The Danger of Medical Misinformation

In Stanley Kubrick's classic 1964 Cold War satire *Dr. Strangelove*, an American general, played by Sterling Hayden, expresses his paranoid fear that fluoridation of the water supply is a Communist plot. Kubrick was poking fun at a right-wing conspiracy theory of that period. But in May 2025 fears about fluoride again made headlines when Texas Republican Attorney General Ken Paxton announced an investigation of leading toothpaste companies Colgate and Procter & Gamble, whose products for children contain the mineral. In a press release, Paxton pointed to a 2024 National Toxicology Program study that suggested fluoride is harming children, in some cases supposedly even lowering IQs. "I will use every tool available to protect our kids from dangerous levels of fluoride exposure and deceptive advertising,"[18] said Paxton. One prominent source, however, rejected Paxton's analysis. The American Dental Association (ADA) stated that fluoride toothpastes have extremely low levels of the substance and that the companies recommend using tiny amounts, pea-sized or smaller, for young children. The ADA also endorsed the benefits of fluoridated water for preventing tooth decay. It called community water fluoridation one of the great health care successes in America, with a positive impact on millions of people.

Nonetheless, Paxton's stance on fluoride's danger to children is shared by officials in the Trump administration, includ-

> "The growing distrust of credible, time-tested, evidence-based science is disheartening. . . . When government officials, like Secretary Kennedy, stand behind the commentary of misinformation and distrust peer-reviewed research it is injurious to public health."[19]
>
> —Brett Kessler, president of the American Dental Association

ing Robert F. Kennedy Jr., head of the US Department of Health and Human Services. In a congressional hearing in May 2025, Kennedy was asked about his recommendation to end the use of fluoridated water across the country. Idaho Representative Mike Simpson, who is also a dentist, told Kennedy that such a move was certain to create a need for more dentists to deal with increased tooth decay. And the dental profession overwhelmingly agrees with Simpson's view. Brett Kessler, president of the ADA, says:

> The growing distrust of credible, time-tested, evidence-based science is disheartening. The myths that fluoridated water is harmful and no longer necessary to prevent dental disease is troublesome and reminds me of fictional plots from old movies like *Dr. Strangelove*. When government officials, like Secretary Kennedy, stand behind the commentary of misinformation and distrust peer-reviewed research it is injurious to public health.[19]

Challenging the Efficacy of Vaccines

Fluoridated water is only one of several issues on which Kennedy's views are disputed by medical experts. He also has led a longtime crusade against vaccines, especially the measles, mumps, and rubella (MMR) vaccine that is administered to children in public schools. Kennedy's anti-vaccine views attracted media scrutiny from the earliest days of the second Trump administration. In late January 2025, an outbreak of measles beginning in West Texas threatened to reverse decades of success in controlling the disease.

Measles is a virus that causes a rash, fever, cough, and runny nose. Although measles can seem like a relatively mild illness, it can lead to serious complications, including pneumonia, encephalitic (brain inflammation), long-term weakness of the immune system, and even death. For most of the 1900s, deaths from measles averaged from five hundred to one thousand a year. The first vaccine for the disease was developed in 1963 by a research team led by John Enders, an American biomedical scientist. In 1971 the measles vaccine was combined with stand-alone vaccines for mumps and rubella to create the MMR version. A widespread, decades-long effort to inoculate children in the United States led to an amazing milestone. In 2000 trackers in America reported no endemic (or community) spread of measles for the previous twelve months. The World Health Organization declared that measles had been eliminated in the United States.

However, fringe critics began to attack the groundbreaking vaccine as dangerous. They pointed to a 1998 study by British physician Andrew Wakefield that claimed the MMR vaccine was linked to autism in children. Concerned scientists performed studies to test Wakefield's claim, but they found no such connection. Later Wakefield was outed as a fraud, having faked data for his paper.

Robert F. Kennedy Jr., pictured speaking at a 2025 Senate hearing, has recommended the end of water fluoridation in the United States, despite disagreement from medical professionals, who worry that this will cause significant harm.

He had hoped to discredit the MMR vaccine so he could make millions with his own vaccine and test kit. In 2010 the journal that had published Wakefield's study finally retracted it, and Wakefield lost his medical license in the United Kingdom. As *New York Times* reporter Susan Dominus wrote in 2011, "Andrew Wakefield has become one of the most reviled doctors of his generation, blamed directly and indirectly, depending on the accuser, for irresponsibly starting a panic with tragic repercussions: vaccination rates so low that childhood diseases once all but eradicated here—whooping cough and measles, among them—have re-emerged, endangering young lives."[20] Since Wakefield's fall from favor, groups like the Centers for Disease Control and Prevention (CDC) and the American Academy of Pediatrics have done exhaustive research on the issue. They have repeatedly debunked claims of any connection between vaccines and autism.

"Andrew Wakefield has become one of the most reviled doctors of his generation, blamed directly and indirectly . . . for irresponsibly starting a panic with tragic repercussions: vaccination rates so low that childhood diseases once all but eradicated here . . . have re-emerged, endangering young lives."[20]

—Susan Dominus, reporter for the *New York Times*

One of Wakefield's early boosters was Robert F. Kennedy Jr. In 2005 Kennedy published an article in *Rolling Stone* that promoted the link between the MMR vaccine and childhood autism. Going forward, Kennedy continued to stoke fears about vaccines through his nonprofit Children's Health Defense. He wrote books and gave numerous interviews that fed a growing skepticism about vaccines. In a 2023 interview, Kennedy denied that the measles vaccine had reduced deaths. He blamed deaths from measles before the vaccine on childhood malnutrition.

Misinformation Contributes to a Measles Outbreak

Medical misinformation, such as the autism scare regarding the MMR vaccine, is especially dangerous to the public because it leads directly to poor health care decisions that affect disease prevention and people's overall health. One example is the mea-

Combating Misinformation About Cancer Treatments

Apple Cider Vinegar, a Netflix drama about a social media influencer's cancer scam, depicts how easily people are fooled by medical misinformation online. The show is based on a ruse perpetuated by Belle Gibson, an Australian influencer who claimed to have cured her brain cancer with natural remedies like apple cider vinegar to lower her body's pH levels. Gibson later admitted she never had cancer and that her story was drummed up to get clicks and views.

Misinformation about cancer treatments has exploded on social media. People who are desperate for options to treat their cancer often turn to social media, especially YouTube, in search of information. What they find is often misleading. Stacy Loeb, professor of urology at New York University, led a study of misinformation about prostate cancer. The study found that 42 percent of the top 150 videos about prostate cancer on YouTube included misinformation. A similar 41 percent of Instagram and TikTok posts included false information. Inaccurate claims can foster distrust among patients and cause a great deal of wasted time during patient visits. As Loeb says, "If we need to discuss the next steps [in treatment] but we spend half of the encounter dispelling myths, that can pose a challenge for providing informed decision-making."

Quoted in Mark Leiser, "Multifaceted Strategy Needed to Combat Cancer Misinformation on Social Media," Healio, September 19, 2024. www.healio.com.

sles outbreak that began in Gaines County, Texas, in early 2025. By March 18 the Texas Department of State Health Services had reported a total of 279 measles cases, close to the nationwide total for all of 2024. Medical officials said most of the patients were either confirmed to be or likely to have been unvaccinated. The CDC noted that vaccination rates were continuing to fall due to misinformation about vaccine safety.

On April 7, with measles cases rising and the disease spreading to other states, Kennedy reversed his longtime position on the MMR vaccine. In a lengthy post on X, he affirmed that it was the most effective way to prevent the spread of measles. Doctors nationwide, who had been concerned about Kennedy's anti-vaccine background, were quick to endorse the change as better late than never. "A single dose [of the MMR vaccine] is roughly 93% effective," said Dr. Paul Offit, director of the Vaccine Education Center at the Children's Hospital of Philadelphia, "and the second dose gets that up to 97%."[21] The Texas Department of

State Health Services reported that only about 2 percent of the 481 measles cases it had recorded as of April 4 were found in individuals who were fully or partially vaccinated. By May 16 the number of confirmed cases had grown to 1,024 in at least thirty states. There were three reported deaths, two of them school-age children.

Medical researchers warn that if MMR vaccination rates do not improve from the current level of 91 percent, the United States could have more than 850,000 measles cases over the next twenty-five years. Some experts have described the United States as being at the tipping point for even more serious outbreaks. Part of the problem has to do with the vaccine's long-term success. Many people today have never seen a case of measles. According to Jason Bowling, an infectious-disease specialist at UT Health San Antonio, "Once it no longer becomes something that people witness, it's harder to get that urgency there."[22]

As for Kennedy's anti-vaccine supporters, some reacted to his pro-vaccine statement with outrage. "I'm sorry, but we voted for

This 2025 photo shows a sign on the door of a Texas medical facility warning about measles. Most cases in the 2025 Texas measles outbreak were believed to be in unvaccinated people.

Wholesale Changes for a Vaccine Advisory Panel

Robert Kennedy Jr., secretary of Health and Human Services, has declared his intention to restore public trust in vaccines. Yet critics say his policies are likely to do just the opposite. In June 2025 Kennedy announced he was replacing all seventeen members of a CDC advisory panel on vaccines. The Advisory Committee on Immunization Practices (ACIP) makes crucial decisions on vaccine policy, including which vaccines are given to children and adults, which shots are covered by insurance, and which are made available for free to children from low-income families. Medical authorities stress that ACIP's work has a powerful effect on Americans' health. Among the purged panel members were some of America's most respected voices on inoculation and vaccine development.

Even more alarming for Kennedy's critics, his first eight replacements on the panel had little experience in vaccine policy. Several are outspoken vaccine skeptics. Sean O'Leary, chair of the Committee on Infectious Diseases for the American Academy of Pediatrics, considers the changes a disaster. "Imagine," he says, "if you took all the air traffic controllers in the U.S. and just fired them and you replaced them with people that not only didn't really know how to be air traffic controllers, but several of them didn't even believe in flying."

Quoted in Maria Godoy, "RFK Jr. Replaced Everyone on the CDC's Vaccine Panel. Here's Why That Matters," *NPR*, June 13, 2025. www.npr.org.

challenging the medical establishment, not parroting it,"[23] posted Texas-based physician Mary Talley Bowden on X. Bowden has also opposed the COVID-19 vaccines and pushed for the use of unproven COVID-19 treatments.

The Persistence of False Information About COVID-19 Vaccines

The COVID-19 vaccines represent another medical success story plagued by misinformation. From the first rollout of the vaccines in December 2020, several fake stories and conspiracy theories arose that undermined people's trust in the shots. The false claims proliferated on social media sites and online platforms. Among the most frequent complaints was that the vaccines were developed too rapidly to ensure their safety. This claim ignored all the clinical trials and safety protocols required for development of vaccines. It also swept past decades of concentrated research on the mRNA technology some vaccines employed. Another false concern was that the COVID-19 vaccines would inflict severe side effects. Some of the wilder claims even predicted that the vaccines would cause infertility, alter a person's DNA, or embed microchips for tracking. Other than mild reactions like fever or soreness, the shots only very rarely produced any serious side effects in patients.

Government health officials and media fact-checking sites like PolitiFact scrambled to debunk the false stories as soon as they appeared. Despite efforts to combat misinformation and deliberate lies, a reluctance to get the original COVID-19 vaccine or the booster proved difficult to address. That hesitancy often was based on partisan political beliefs, such as right-wing distrust of the federal government, and not medical evidence. Studies and surveys showed a distinct partisan divide in vaccination rates. In 2022 the Brookings Institution, a left-leaning think tank, found that 90 percent of Democrats were vaccinated against COVID-19 compared to only 58 percent of Republicans. Researchers claim that this disparity led to higher death rates for those who refused to get the vaccine. One study found that conservative counties had death rates from the virus that were almost three times higher than more liberal counties.

False information about COVID-19 vaccines refuses to go away. According to a July 2024 health survey from the University of Pennsylvania's Annenberg Public Policy Center, more than 25 percent of Americans falsely believe that COVID-19 vaccines have caused thousands of deaths. More than 20 percent adhere to the incorrect idea that getting a COVID-19 infection is less hazardous than getting the vaccine. The data indicates that misinformation about COVID-19 vaccines has increased, making people less likely to get the shot.

Misusing Reports of Vaccine Deaths

Efforts by the CDC to find and investigate possible concerns about the COVID vaccines have been used by vaccine opponents to spread more misinformation and confusion. For example, in the two years prior to December 2022, the CDC received 18,007 reports of people dying after receiving the COVID-19 vaccine. The reports went through the Vaccine Adverse Event Reporting System (VAERS), which is run jointly by the CDC and the US Food and Drug Administration. Submitted reports do not prove that deaths resulted from getting the COVID-19 vaccine. Instead, they provide cases for government health officials to investigate.

Nonetheless, vaccine skeptics and anti-vax activists have tried to use the unsubstantiated VAERS reports to discredit COVID-19 vaccines. For example, in January 2023 Peter McCullough, a Dallas, Texas–based cardiologist and aggressive vaccine critic, falsely claimed that thousands of people had died as a result of vaccination against COVID-19. "The vaccine is killing people," McCullough said in a video clip on Instagram. "And it's killing large numbers of people. . . . Our CDC, as of December 23, 2022, has over 16,000 Americans that have died within a few days of taking the vaccine and that's probably a gross underreport."[24]

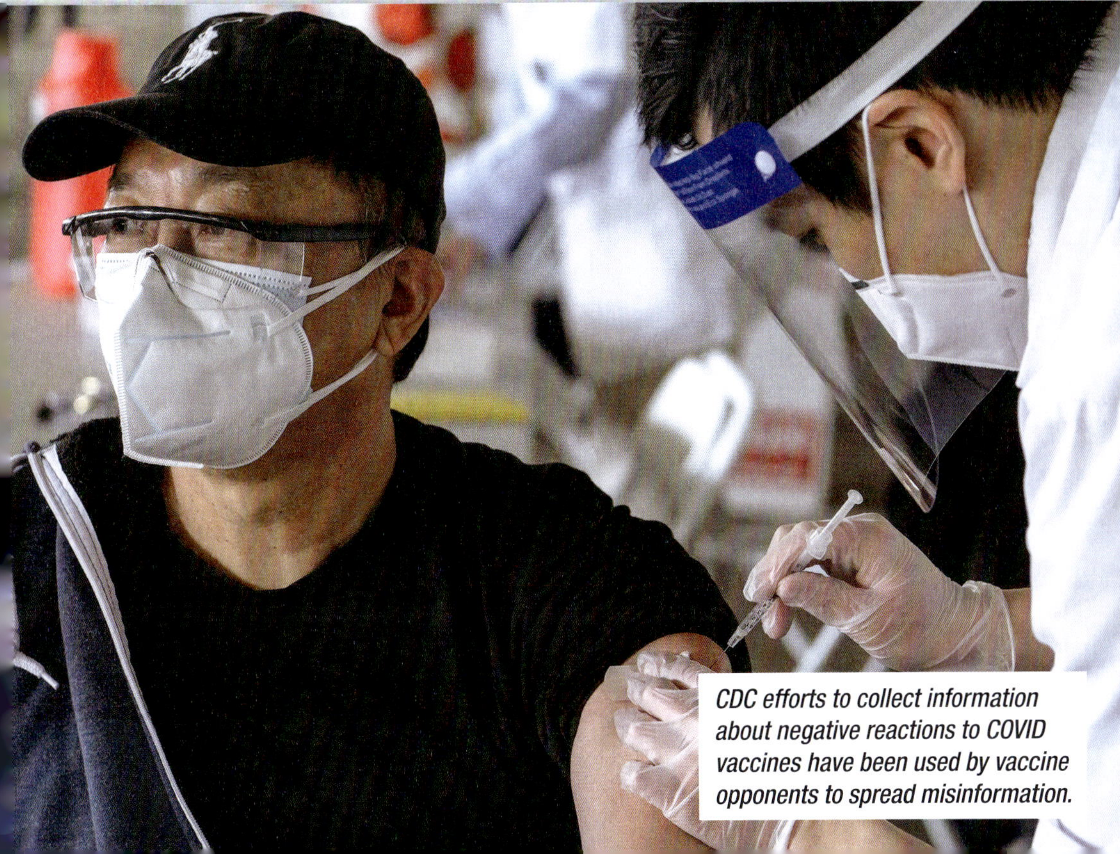

CDC efforts to collect information about negative reactions to COVID vaccines have been used by vaccine opponents to spread misinformation.

What McCullough and other critics do not say is that the numerous VAERS reports are unverified. They may include information that is inaccurate, incomplete, coincidental, or impossible to substantiate. For instance, if an elderly person in failing health dies several days after getting the vaccine, that death is more likely due to natural causes than reaction to the vaccine. In fact, when McCullough made his Instagram post, the CDC's investigations had confirmed only nine deaths resulting from COVID-19 vaccines. These were all linked to statistically rare blood clots produced by the Johnson & Johnson version of the vaccine, and its use in the United States was halted in 2021. As Jason Salemi, associate professor of epidemiology at the University of South Florida, says, "When clinicians have actually reviewed death certificates, autopsy details, and medical records, an exceedingly small number of deaths has been deemed to be causally associated with the vaccine."[25]

"When clinicians have actually reviewed death certificates, autopsy details, and medical records, an exceedingly small number of deaths has been deemed to be causally associated with the [COVID-19] vaccine."[25]

—Jason Salemi, associate professor of epidemiology at the University of South Florida

Misinformation and conspiracy theories about health care issues such as water fluoridation and vaccines can have devastating effects on the health and well-being of people from all age groups. Medical professionals stress how important it is for government agencies and officials to provide reliable, fact-based information about health care and refute false claims before they spread.

CHAPTER FOUR

Conspiracy Theories and Potential Violence

On July 13, 2024, with tensions running high in the months before the upcoming presidential election, a lone gunman tried to assassinate former President Donald Trump as he spoke onstage at an outdoor campaign rally in Butler, Pennsylvania. The shooter was a twenty-year-old Pennsylvania man named Thomas Crooks. One bullet wounded Trump in his upper right ear and almost certainly would have killed him—on live TV—had he not moved his head slightly at the last moment. Other shots killed one audience member, fifty-year-old former fire chief Corey Comperatore, and left two others critically injured. Images of a bloodied Trump surrounded by Secret Service agents and defiantly raising his fist in the air went viral in minutes.

After the attack, conservative pundits questioned how the Secret Service and local police could have allowed an assassin armed with a high-powered rifle to position himself on a nearby rooftop and fire eight rounds before being shot and killed himself. They noted that rally attendees on the outer reaches of the grounds had pointed out Crooks to law enforcement officers as he crouched atop a metal storage building. Anti-Trump skeptics (sometimes called BlueAnon, as the left-wing equivalent of the right-wing QAnon conspiracy theorists) had their own suspicions. They immediately suggested that the assassination attempt had been staged to win public sympathy.

A thorough investigation provided few answers. It found Crooks to be a loner with no identifiable motive for the attack. There was evidence that he had also looked up President Joe Biden's campaign schedule, perhaps contemplating an attack on Biden. As one federal official told CNN, "Even though he didn't get his primary target, the shooter was successful in a lot of ways because he got closer to doing something no one has done in decades."[26]

Eruptions of Violence and Violent Imagery in the Trump Era

Fears about further violence during the campaign nearly came true. The assassination attempt in Butler was followed by another alleged attempt just two months later. On September 15, 2024, a gunman armed with an AK-47 equipped with a scope was spotted by a Secret Service agent on the grounds of Trump International Golf Club in West Palm Beach, Florida. Ryan Wesley Routh, the would-be assassin, was concealed in some bushes only about 300 to 500 yards (274 m to 457 m) from Trump, who was playing golf. The agent immediately opened fire on Routh, who ran to his nearby vehicle and tried to escape down an access road. He was stopped by police and arrested shortly thereafter.

Once again, questions arose about how a potential assassin was able to get within firing range of the former president. Secret Service protocol called for a wide sweep of the golf course grounds to guard against potential threats. Investigations into Routh's background provided more grist for conspiracy theorists. Investigators found that Routh had tried to acquire weapons to shoot down Trump's plane. "Send me an rpg [rocket propelled grenade] or stinger and I will see what we can do," he allegedly told an associate. "I need equipment so that Trump cannot get elected."[27] Obsessed with the Ukraine crisis, he had tried to recruit volunteers to fight for Ukraine in its war against Russia. Right-wing commentators speculated, with no evidence, that Routh must have had ties to the US military and may have played a role in a larger, government-backed assassination plot. "What are the odds that this shooter, who spent months fighting in Ukraine, has zero links to anyone in US military or intelligence circles?" wrote Charlie Kirk, the founder of conservative nonprofit Turning Point USA, on X. "Find them."[28]

The two assassination attempts on Trump prompted conservatives to recall other incidents and imagery that seemed, in their view, to declare open season on the former president. Some looked back to Trump's first term. In May 2017 comedian Kathy Griffin posted a photo online of her holding a mock severed head of Trump. A few weeks later a controversial spoof of Shakespeare's *Julius Caesar* at New York City's Central Park featured an actor in a Trump mask as Caesar. When the Roman dictator fell to the knives of the assassins in the play, many in the audience cheered. These incidents certainly received pushback at the time. Despite her subsequent apology, Griffin's career was derailed. New York's Shakespeare in the Park company had to deal with protesters, disruptions of the play, and media criticism in some circles.

Early in Trump's second term, another potential implication of violence came from an unexpected source. In May 2025 former Federal Bureau of Investigation (FBI) Director James Comey posted

Donald Trump arrives for a campaign rally in Butler, Pennsylvania, on July 13, 2024. He was wounded in the ear in an assassination attempt during the rally.

on Instagram a photo of seashells on the beach that formed the number 8647. Comey described it as a "cool shell formation on my beach walk."[29] But many observers interpreted the photo to mean *eighty-six* (slang for "kill" or "cancel") *forty-seven* (meaning Trump, as the forty-seventh US president). Comey quickly deleted the post and claimed not to have seen any negative connotation to the numbers.

Plots and Conspiracies Fueled by Violent Rhetoric

In the run-up to the 2020 US elections, a kidnapping plot in Michigan arose in response to that state's COVID-19 lockdown policies. Michigan's governor, Democrat Gretchen Whitmer, had drawn national attention for implementing some of the country's strictest measures to deal with the pandemic. These included lockdowns, stay-at-home orders, forced closings of businesses, and mandated social distancing. Whitmer's supporters said her prevention strategy was necessary to protect the public. Opponents accused her

Normalizing Extremist Views

In May 2025 the Southern Poverty Law Center (SPLC) reported a significant decrease in the number of antigovernment, White nationalist, and other extremist groups in the United States. In its annual *Year in Hate and Extremism* report, the SPLC said it counted 1,371 hate and extremist groups nationwide in 2024. This was compared to 1,430 groups in 2023. However, the report stressed that the drop did not mean the influence of such extremist views was declining. Instead, people who share these beliefs see their viewpoints becoming increasingly mainstream in America.

Apparently, the 5 percent decrease in the number of groups in 2024 was due to a lack of motivation for extremists to organize. They believe their radical agenda in politics, education, and social issues has mostly been adopted by the Trump administration. For example, Trump's crusade to end diversity, equity, and inclusion initiatives aligns with many antigovernment viewpoints. The extremist groups addressed in the 2025 report are part of the far-right movement that targets women, immigrants, and minorities, according to Rachel Carroll, SPLC Intelligence Project's interim director. As Carroll notes, "Their power comes from the use of force, the capture of political parties and government, and infesting the mainstream discourse with conspiracy theories."

Quoted in Léonie Chao-Fong, "Number of US White Nationalist Groups Falls as Extremist Views Go Mainstream," *The Guardian* (US edition), May 22, 2025. www.theguardian.com.

After her strict COVID-19 lockdown policies were criticized by Trump, Michigan's governor, Democrat Gretchen Whitmer, was targeted in a kidnapping plot.

of seizing too much power as governor and making up her policies on the fly. "Whitmer's make-it-up-as-you-go approach damaged the public's trust in another way," says Michael Van Beek, director of research at the Mackinac Center for Public Policy. "She reversed herself often, mandating one policy one day and then abandoning it in the next order. It became a sort of mystery science, where one could only guess at the slippery rationales the governor used to make her decisions."[30] In effect, said opponents, she was ordering a large-scale quarantine, not of the sick but of healthy people, something that rarely if ever had been tried before.

Trump criticized Whitmer's policies as too restrictive, socially disruptive, and antibusiness. In mid-April he posted the tweet "LIBERATE MICHIGAN!,"[31] which many in the national media interpreted as a call to arms for extremists. Two weeks later, a crowd of gun-carrying right-wing protesters assembled at the Michigan capitol building. They managed to invade the capitol in what was later seen as a preview of the January 6 riot by Trump supporters in Washington, DC. The Michigan uprising ended with no one being injured. But the incident left the state's citizenry fearful and uncertain of what might follow.

Four of the armed protesters, along with other militia members, were arrested in October 2020 for their role in a tangled plot to kidnap and perhaps even murder Whitmer. The militia group, known as the Wolverine Watchmen, had been monitored for months by FBI agents looking for possible violent extremists. Prosecutors said that the antigovernment conspirators, numbering thirteen in all, planned to kidnap Whitmer at her Michigan vacation home in Mackinac Island. They hoped that seizing the governor would ignite a civil war in the weeks before the November election. After the plot was revealed, Whitmer accused Trump of contributing to the potential violence with his rhetoric. "When our leaders speak, their words matter. They carry weight," she said. "When they stoke and contribute to hate speech, they are complicit."[32]

"When our leaders speak, their words matter. They carry weight. . . . When they stoke and contribute to hate speech, they are complicit."[32]

—Gretchen Whitmer, Michigan governor

The Alt-Right and Its Reliance on Conspiracy Theories

Militia groups like the Wolverine Watchmen share many beliefs with the so-called alternative right, or alt-right, movement in the United States. The alt-right arose in the late 2000s as a loose association of White nationalists and far-right opponents of feminism, globalism, and immigration. Alt-right groups are mostly made up of relatively young White males. They tend to reject traditional conservative views in favor of a more radical, often racially based agenda. The alt-right's reliance on conspiracy theories and threats of violence have drawn attention from the FBI and other law enforcement agencies. Critics of the alt-right movement consider it an expression of White supremacy. In August 2017, during Trump's first term, a Unite the Right rally in Charlottesville, Virginia, saw hundreds of neo-Nazis, right-wing militias, and other alt-right factions facing off against anti-fascist counterprotesters. At one point, a truck driven by an alt-right supporter plowed into the anti-fascist group, killing one woman and injuring a dozen others.

A Political Murder and Its Aftermath

Early on the morning of December 4, 2024, Brian Thompson, chief executive officer of United Healthcare, was gunned down on the street in New York City. Thompson had just arrived for a corporate meeting at a downtown hotel when a lone gunman fired multiple shots into the victim's back. The attack turned out to be a political murder of sorts. Twenty-seven-year-old Luigi Mangione, the alleged shooter, was later arrested in Pennsylvania. He claimed in a written manifesto to be acting against the health insurance industry and its conspiracy to defraud customers by denying payment for care. News reports said that Mangione had battled severe back pain for years and blamed companies like United Healthcare for his failure to get relief.

What happened next was almost as shocking as the murder. Many people on social media expressed support for Mangione and showed little sympathy for Thompson, a husband and father. Pictures of Mangione were posted repeatedly, along with messages of solidarity for his views about medical insurers. "It's hard to interpret for every individual what these memes mean to them," says Cliff Lampe, professor of information at the University of Michigan, "but in general they seem to represent a frustration with perceived inequities in the healthcare system."

Quoted in Peter Suciu, "Luigi Mangione Has Become a Social Media Folk Hero," *Forbes*, December 12, 2024. www.forbes.com.

After the rally, the discredited alt-right collapsed as a movement. However, its poisonous views on race, gender equality, and immigration continue to influence far-right extremists in America.

In 2016 the website 4chan, which had hosted many early alt-right figures, gave birth to a hub for right-wing conspiracy theories, called QAnon. Launched by a YouTube creator and two moderators of 4chan, QAnon featured posts and videos that claimed to be intelligence leaks. One conspiracy theory described, with no evidence, how Trump was fighting a secret war against a criminal faction made up of politicians and Hollywood elites. Supposedly, the insiders were engaged in devil worship and child molestation. These wild tales came to a head in a conspiracy theory dubbed Pizzagate. In December 2016 a QAnon believer armed with an assault rifle stormed into a pizza restaurant in Washington, DC, and opened fire, reportedly to stop what he believed was a child-sex ring operating there. No one was injured, and the man was sentenced to four years in prison.

Following the incident, authorities stepped up their investigations of QAnon and its links to possible violence. The FBI has released reports classifying QAnon as a source of fringe beliefs that can motivate extremists to commit violent acts and engage in other criminal behavior. QAnon followers have been implicated in assassination plots, felony threats, aggravated assaults, kidnapping, armed standoffs with law enforcement, and even the setting of wildfires in Southern California. At least thirty-four QAnon figures took part in the Capitol riot on January 6. Among them was Jacob Chansley, the so-called QAnon Shaman. Chansley, wearing red, white, and blue face paint and a bearskin headdress with horns, was later convicted of entering the Senate Chamber and leaving a threatening note for then-vice president Mike Pence.

Related groups have also promoted conspiracy theories that can lead to violence. The Proud Boys are a right-wing extremist group with a history of street brawls and targeted harassment of left-wing political foes. According to the Anti-Defamation League, the group maintains nearly 150 chapters in the United States, Canada, Australia, and other nations. To join the group, candidates must go through four degrees of membership, first swearing an oath of loyalty: "I'm a proud Western chauvinist, I refuse to apologize for creating the modern world."[33] To achieve the highest degree, members must engage in a conflict for the cause or get arrested fighting leftists. The Proud Boys have pushed conspiracy theories about stolen elections and left-wing plots to form a world government. Four leaders of the Proud Boys were convicted of seditious conspiracy, or plotting to overthrow the federal government, for their role in the January 6 Capitol riot. More recently, in September 2024 the Proud Boys staged a demonstration against Haitian immigrants in Springfield, Ohio. They also share crowdfunding campaigns with right-wing militia groups like the Oath Keepers and Three Percenters.

"I'm a proud Western chauvinist, I refuse to apologize for creating the modern world."[33]

—Loyalty oath of the Proud Boys, a right-wing extremist group

The Proud Boys, pictured here in Washington, DC, in 2020, have pushed conspiracy theories about stolen elections and left-wing plots to form a world government.

An Uneasy Postelection Period

Although the 2024 election proceeded without violence or widespread protests, the postelection period was marked by unease for many Americans. Anonymous bomb threats and swatting attempts targeted members of Congress from both parties as well as some Trump administration appointees. John S. Hollywood of the RAND Corporation, a research group on public policy issues, believes that anxiety about civil war and mass political violence in America is almost certainly overblown. However, he does admit that both political sides harbor fears about what the other side could do to the nation if given enough power. "While the specifics differ, too many on both sides of the political divide agreed that the opposing party would usher in an authoritarian regime," says Hollywood. "One poll [from NBC News in 2024] found that over two-thirds of respondents, regardless of party, felt that the other party's agenda 'poses a threat that if not stopped will destroy America as we know it.'"[34]

This polarized, paranoid mindset on the part of so many Americans makes the spread of conspiracy theories even more dangerous. Security experts and law enforcement officials agree that combating misinformation and conspiracy theories will be a crucial task in the years ahead.

CHAPTER FIVE

Controlling the Spread of Misinformation

As misinformation online spreads more quickly than ever before, some politicians want governments to exert greater control over speech. In November 2024, for example, Minnesota Attorney General Keith Ellison was defending a new state law that banned the use of deepfake technology—or AI-created fake images—to influence elections. Conservatives were challenging the law in federal court as a violation of the First Amendment and its protection of free speech. To defend the law, Ellison turned to Jeff Hancock, director of the Stanford Social Media Lab and an expert on how technology is used for deception. Hancock's brief for the court cited several academic sources in defense of the anti-deepfake law. However, as the opposing legal team pointed out, two of Hancock's sources were themselves fake. One study, titled "The Influence of Deepfake Videos on Political Attitudes and Behavior," did not appear in the journal that was cited. It and another article in Hancock's brief were apparently so-called AI hallucinations generated erroneously by a large language model such as ChatGPT. As Frank Bednarz, lead attorney for the plaintiffs, told the judge, "By calling out the AI-generated fabrication to the court, we demonstrate that the best remedy for false speech remains true speech—not censorship."[35]

Using AI to Identify Fake News and Disinformation

AI doubtlessly contributes to misinformation, both by creating deepfakes to fool people and occasionally fabricating fictitious references, like Hancock's bogus articles. However, AI experts note that the technology also can play an important role in identifying fake news and deliberate disinformation. Such a capability is crucial to eliminating false content online and restoring trust for users. According to the 2024 *Global Risks Report* from the World Economic Forum, disinformation is the main challenge facing the world today and is likely to be a menacing problem for the next decade.

For example, recent studies show that AI's machine learning outperforms humans in detecting when people's statements veer from accepted facts. Researchers at the University of California, San Diego, Rady School of Management used tapes of a British game show called *Golden Balls* to test subjects' ability to spot deliberate lies made by the show's human contestants in response to given questions. The AI algorithms correctly flagged contestants' responses as truthful or deceptive 74 percent of the time. This compared to a 51 to 53 percent rate of accuracy for the six hundred humans in the study who assessed the players' responses.

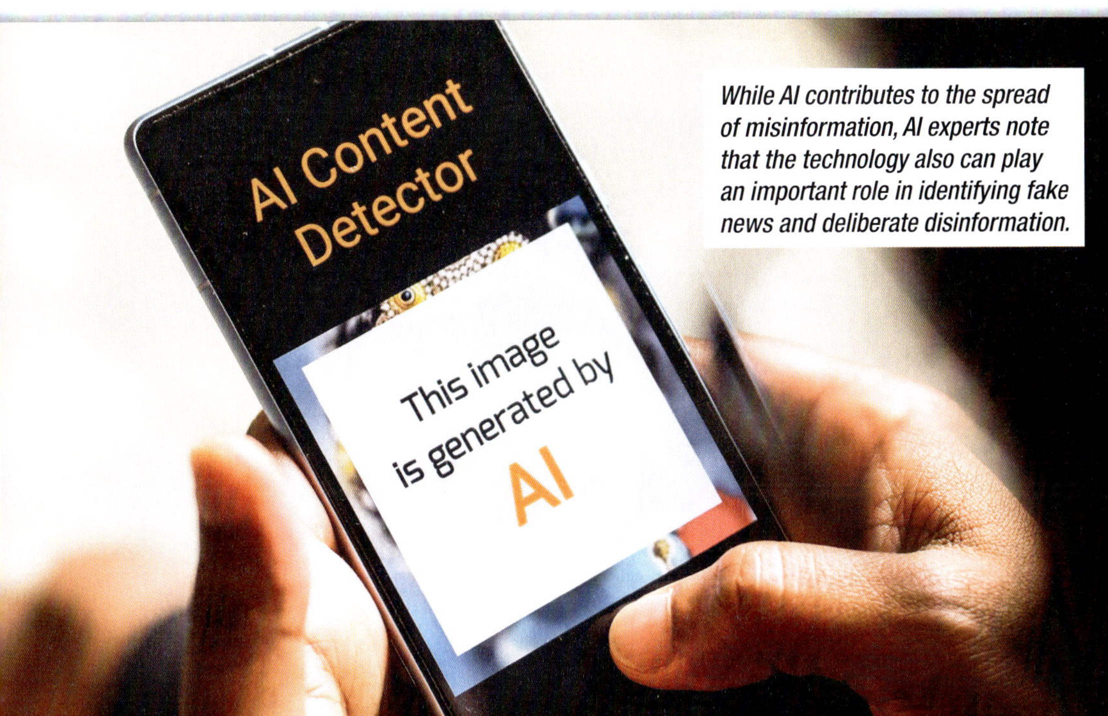

While AI contributes to the spread of misinformation, AI experts note that the technology also can play an important role in identifying fake news and deliberate disinformation.

> **"We find that there are certain 'tells' when a person is being deceptive. . . . Algorithms work better at uncovering these correlations."[36]**
>
> —Marta Serra-Garcia, lead author of a University of California, San Diego study on detecting lies with AI

"We find that there are certain 'tells' when a person is being deceptive," says Marta Serra-Garcia, lead author of the study. "For example, if someone is happier, they are telling the truth and there are other visual, verbal, vocal cues that we as humans share when we are being honest and telling the truth. Algorithms work better at uncovering these correlations."[36] The study also suggests that AI can assist users in finding the truth on their own. Using the AI flags as a guide to who was lying helped the human subjects improve their own evaluations. Researchers say this shows how AI could help people recognize false or deceptive content on platforms like YouTube, TikTok, and Instagram.

Google has expanded its AI system for identifying and marking AI-generated material. The company's latest line of SynthID technology adds watermarks to video and text that is AI-generated. The watermarks enable AI-produced material to be traced back to its original source. Identifying source content as fake or intentionally misleading helps prevent disinformation from being shared or spread. Google also offers its SynthID text watermarking as an open-source system for other vendors to use. The company is constantly trying to improve the technology. "We test our own models and try to break them by identifying weaknesses," says James Manyika, senior vice president at Google. "Building AI responsibility means both addressing the risks and maximizing the benefits of people and society."[37]

According to the World Economic Forum (WEF), a key problem of the modern age is how disinformation travels much faster than the truth. Advanced AI-driven systems can help solve this problem by weeding out disinformation on websites and in social media posts. AI content detectors use machine learning to inspect syntax and sentence structures to determine whether text is AI-generated or written by a person. AI can also rapidly compare information with reliable sources, enabling it to flag content that might include deliberate falsehoods.

Using Machine Learning to Detect Conspiracy Theories Online

Sharing conspiracy theories on social media causes direct public harm by shifting discussions away from facts and analysis. Yet it is difficult for social media platforms to identify conspiracy theories before they can spread. Google's Jigsaw unit is dedicated to stopping conspiracy threats with new technology, such as machine learning. Working with researchers at the RAND Corporation, the Jigsaw unit has developed a machine learning program to detect the special language of conspiracy theories. The program searches for rhetoric typically found in posts that promote conspiracy theories. This experimental model offers the opportunity to detect conspiratorial language before its ideas go viral.

Another way to undermine misinformation and conspiracy theories is to inoculate online users against the lies before they see them. A separate Jigsaw group worked with a team from two British universities to engage in so-called prebunking. Users are shown ninety-second animated videos detailing the tactics used to spread misinformation. According to the team's report, users were much more skeptical of conspiratorial claims after seeing the videos. According to Beth Goldberg, head of research and development at Jigsaw, "This is one of the few misinformation interventions that I've seen at least that has worked not just across the conspiratorial spectrum but across the political spectrum."

Quoted in Nico Grant and Tiffany Hsu, "Google Finds 'Inoculating' People Against Misinformation Helps Blunt Its Power," *New York Times*, August 24, 2022. www.nytimes.com.

AI content detectors are not foolproof, however. Research shows that their success rate is about 70 percent. But they are still in the early stages of development, and they are already helping restore users' trust in media content. Schools and universities are using them to identify AI-generated material in class assignments. The WEF promotes the use of AI content-detecting tools to identify and combat disinformation. At the same time, its Global Coalition for Digital Safety also recommends that people strive to become more media literate to recognize signs of fake news and disinformation online. Schools, libraries, and community groups can help people develop media literacy skills beginning at a young age. Such skills include evaluating information sources, recognizing disinformation and propaganda, and making informed decisions about media content. In fact, experts contend that battling the spread of disinformation calls for a joint effort of governments, media companies, tech firms, and individuals in society.

The Global Campaign Against Disinformation

The campaign to stop the spread of disinformation and conspiracy theories has become one of today's key global issues. Many nations have debated new laws that would give their governments increased authority to censor content considered to be misleading or hateful. Beginning in October 2022, the European Commission, the governing body of the European Union, passed new laws to address disinformation and hate speech on the internet. The laws did not take full effect until February 2024. They were intended to protect Europe's democracies from foreign interference, especially from Russia and China, in the run-up to elections in June 2024. Ursula von der Leyen, the president of the European Commission, called the effort the European Democracy Shield. "I believe Europe now needs its own dedicated structure for countering foreign interference," she said. "It will pool the necessary expertise and link up and coordinate with existing national agencies."[38]

> **"I believe Europe now needs its own dedicated structure for countering foreign interference [on social media]. It will pool the necessary expertise and link up and coordinate with existing national agencies."[38]**
>
> —Ursula von der Leyen, president of the European Commission

One of the new laws, the Digital Services Act (DSA), set up a strict rulebook for social media companies to follow in the fight against disinformation and conspiracy theories. The DSA requires companies with at least 45 million monthly users to take strong measures to control the spread of hate speech, misinformation, and terrorist propaganda. For example, Meta, which owns Facebook and Instagram, was placed under investigation for potential violations of the DSA's digital rulebook in its handling of misinformation. Another law, the Code of Practice on Disinformation, seeks to impose large financial penalties on sources of disinformation. It also aims to improve the transparency of online advertising and empower users to detect false or misleading content. EU countries also planned to establish so-called Hybrid Rapid Response Teams to deal with cyber threats. Such threats might include foreign governments manipulating information, creating disinformation, and interfering in elections.

Calls for laws and rules to combat disinformation raise concerns about government censorship and free speech.

Some social media heads protested that the European Commission's new laws amounted to government censorship. However, those who believe disinformation and conspiracy theories require strong measures to stop their spread were pleased with the laws. In a September 2024 speech to EU officials at a WEF event, former US Secretary of State John Kerry praised the initiatives. Kerry also remarked on how difficult it is to pass similar laws in the United States. As he told the EU audience:

> You know there's a lot of discussion now about how you curb those [social media companies] in order to guarantee that you're going to have some accountability on facts, etc. But look, if people only go to one source, and the source they go to is sick, and, you know, has an agenda, and they're putting out disinformation, our First Amendment stands as a major block to be able to just, you know, hammer it out of existence. . . . Democracies around the world now are struggling with the absence of a sort of truth arbiter, and there's no one who defines what facts really are.[39]

Combating Disinformation Versus Censorship Concerns

Kerry's remarks served to highlight a major issue in governments' attempts to restrain the spread of fake news and disinformation. The calls for laws and rules to combat disinformation also raised concerns about government censorship and free speech. Conservative critics claimed that Kerry seemed to oppose the First Amendment. Liberal supporters insisted that Kerry was simply pointing out how difficult it is to balance the policing of social media with protection of speech rights. There was also disagreement about whether the government should stand as the "truth arbiter," deciding what is true and what is not. Skeptics worried that giving governments this authority would lead to censorship of disfavored viewpoints, especially those that criticize the government.

These concerns surfaced again when the European Union reportedly planned to pursue legal action against Elon Musk and X, his social media company formerly known as Twitter. According to reports in April 2025, EU officials were preparing to hit X with large fines for violating the DSA. The European Union charged Musk's company with allowing illicit content and disinformation to go unchecked. In seeking to make an example of X, the European Union was prepared to levy fines of more than $1 billion for all the company's alleged violations. In addition, the European Union was demanding changes to X's policies about user-generated content and hate speech. It also insisted that X must become more transparent in how it polices its platform and controls its content. A statement from the European Commission said, "We have always enforced and will continue to enforce our laws fairly and without discrimination toward all companies operating in the E.U., in full compliance with global rules."[40]

Musk responded to the proposed penalties by labeling them a violation of free speech. This followed Vice President J.D. Vance's February 2025 speech to EU officials in which Vance compared the DSA and other EU media regulations to digital censorship. Musk's alliance with Trump and the Trump administration seemed

Using Deepfakes to Spread Disinformation

Students today find themselves living through what some experts call an "infodemic," a torrent of information that spreads like a viral disease. Unfortunately, much of this information is false or intentionally misleading. "There is nonstop misinformation from all sides, everywhere, 24/7," says Eugene Kiely, executive director of FactCheck.org. "Misinformation used to be more cyclical and tied to elections, but there is no lull in misinformation now."

Educators are seeking to equip students to navigate this sea of data. States such as California, Illinois, New Jersey, and Texas have mandatory programs to teach students media literacy and the skills for identifying reliable information. For example, the News Literacy Project helps students develop media literacy skills by connecting them to professional journalists. The program, called Newsroom to Classroom, enlists journalist volunteers to visit schools or meet with students virtually to discuss misinformation, disinformation, the media's role as watchdog, and First Amendment issues. "Teachers find it helpful because it humanizes journalism and gives students an opportunity to engage with real journalists and ask them questions," says Brittney Smith, who manages school district partnerships for the program. "It's never too early to talk to kids about media literacy and disinformation."

Quoted in Cindy Long, "Helping Students Spot Misinformation Online," *NEA Today*, October 17, 2024. www.nea.org.

to frame the debate as a standoff between the United States and the European Union over how to deal with misinformation and misleading content. A White House memo accused the European Union of targeting American social media companies unfairly.

Questions About the Future of Fact-Checking

While the European Union has sought to tighten regulations of social media companies, the American-based giants have reduced their reliance on fact-checking and control of content. Beginning in December 2016 after Trump's first election victory, Facebook contracted with FactCheck.org, PolitiFact, the Associated Press, ABC News, and other fact-checking outfits to control misinformation on its platform. Facebook fact-checkers were especially active during the run-up to the 2020 election and the subsequent accusations of fraud. But in January 2025, Meta, which owns Facebook and Instagram, ended its agreement with third-party fact-checkers. Instead, it laid out plans to rely on a user-based fact-checking system that it called Community Notes. This system was similar to changes Musk had made at X. "We've reached a point where it's just too many mistakes and too much censorship," Meta CEO Mark Zuckerberg said in announcing the new policy. "The recent elections also feel like a cultural tipping point towards, once again, prioritizing speech. So, we're going to get back to our roots and focus on reducing mistakes, simplifying our policies, and restoring free expression on our platforms."[41] However, Zuckerberg admitted that, due to the changes, "we're going to catch less bad stuff."[42]

The Meta announcement sent fact-checking outlets scrambling and wondering about their future. Media analysts also questioned whether social media platforms would become a sort of free-for-all situation in which false stories and disinformation were enabled instead of flagged. Some saw Zuckerberg's about-face as a betrayal. "To blame fact-checkers is a disappointing cop-out," said Neil Brown of the Poynter Institute, which owns PolitiFact. "Facts are not censorship. Fact-checkers never censored anything. And Meta always held the cards."[43]

Efforts to identify and eliminate false stories, disinformation, and conspiracy theories online have met with concerns about censorship and protecting free speech. Finding the right balance is a constant challenge for social media sites and message board administrators. This seems likely to remain a problem in today's politically fractured America.

SOURCE NOTES

Introduction: Trading in False Information

1. Quoted in Anthony L. Fisher, "This 'Historian' Won MAGA Fame as a Big Lie Apologist. Now, He's Defends Nazis," Yahoo! News, September 7, 2024. www.yahoo.com.
2. Abe Greenwald, "Joe Rogan Isn't Openminded—He's Bad," *Commentary*, March 14, 2025. www.commentary.org.
3. Fay M. Johnson, "Ye and the Limits of Free Speech Online," *New York Times*, February 19, 2025. www.nytimes.com.

Chapter One: How Misinformation and Conspiracy Theories Spread

4. Quoted in Laura Doan and Erielle Delzer, "Wildflower Conspiracy Theories Are Going Viral Again. Why?," CBS News, January 16, 2025. www.cbsnews.com.
5. Quoted in *Business Wire*, "Most Americans View Conspiracy Theories as Dangerous, Despite Nearly 50% Believing Alien Visits Were Covered Up by the Government," November 20, 2023. www.businesswire.com.
6. Quoted in Christina A. Cassidy and Christine Fernando, "Election Officials Are Fighting a Tsunami of Voting Conspiracy Theories," Associated Press, October 23, 2024. https://apnews.com.
7. Miah Hammond-Errey, "Elon Musk's Twitter Is Becoming a Sewer of Disinformation," *Foreign Policy*, July 15, 2023. https://foreignpolicy.com.
8. Nicole Gill, "Accountable Tech Condemns Meta's Decision to End Fact Checking: Gut Trust and Safety Measures," Accountable Tech, 2025. https://accountabletech.org.
9. Emily Harding, "A Russian Bot Farm Used AI to Lie to Americans. What Now?," Center for Strategic and International Studies, July 16, 2024. www.csis.org.
10. Quoted in Matt Burgess and Lily Hay Newman, "Suspected 4chan Hack Could Expose Longtime, Anonymous Admins," *Wired*, April 15, 2025. www.wired.com.

Chapter Two: Elections and Conspiracy Theories

11. Quoted in Kimberlee Kruesi and Sarah Brumfield, "Witnesses Saw an Armed Group Harassing Aid Workers in a Small Tennessee Town, Sheriff Says," Associated Press, October 21, 2024. https://apnews.com.
12. Quoted in Jamie Whitehead, "FEMA Official Ordered Storm Crews Not to Help Trump Voters," BBC, November 9, 2024. www.bbc.com.
13. Quoted in Robert Yoon, "Trump's Drumbeat of Lies About the 2020 Election Keeps Getting Louder. Here Are the Facts," Associated Press, August 27, 2023. https://apnews.com.
14. Molly Ball, "The Secret History of the Shadow Campaign That Saved the 2020 Election," *Time*, February 4, 2021. www.time.com.
15. Quoted in Sara Murray et al., "Election Officials Are Hustling to Fight Misinformation in Real Time as Early Voting Begins," *CNN,* October 22, 2024. www.cnn.com.
16. Quoted in Andrew Kiser, "'Threatening' Package Intercepted, Addressed to Colorado Secretary of State's Office," Western Slope Now, September 17, 2024. www.westernslopenow.com.
17. Quoted in Christina A. Cassidy, "From Panic Buttons to Bulletproof Glass, U.S. Election Officials Are Preparing for Threats," PBS, September 17, 2024. www.pbs.org.

Chapter Three: The Danger of Medical Misinformation

18. Quoted in Angela Lim, "Paxton Joins RFK's Anti-Fluoride Crusade, Targeting 'Misleading, Deceptive, and Dangerous' Kids' Toothpaste," *Barbed Wire*, May 2, 2025. https://thebarbedwire.com.
19. Quoted in American Dental Association, "Making America Healthy Means Keeping Water Fluoridated," April 7, 2025. www.ada.org.
20. Susan Dominus, "The Crash and Burn of an Autism Guru," *New York Times*, April 20, 2011. www.nytimes.com.
21. Quoted in Geoff Brumfel, "Health Secretary RFK Jr. Endorses the MMR Vaccine—Stoking Fury Among His Supporters," NPR, April 7, 2025. www.npr.org.
22. Quoted in Jennifer Calfas, "The U.S. Eliminated Measles in 2000. The Texas Outbreak Could Upend That," *Wall Street Journal*, April 30, 2025. www.wsj.com.

23. Mary Talley Bowden MD (@MdBreathe), "So we're talking about freedom here. Where is the line? Because mRNA, shouldn't it be left up to the person to decide if they want that or not?" X, April 6, 2025, 3:04 p.m., https://x.com/MdBreathe/status/1908974085108883705.
24. Quoted in Melissa Goldin, "Posts Mischaracterize CDC Data on COVID-19 Vaccine Deaths," Associated Press, January 11, 2023. https://apnews.com.
25. Quoted in Goldin, "Posts Mischaracterize CDC Data on COVID-19 Vaccine Deaths."

Chapter Four: Conspiracy Theories and Potential Violence

26. Quoted in Zachary Cohen et al., "Investigators Piece Together a Puzzling Portrait of the Shooter Who Sought to Assassinate Trump," CNN, July 19, 2024. www.cnn.com.
27. Quoted in Jacob Rosen and Scott McFarlane, "Trump's Would-Be Assassin Ryan Routh Sought Weapon to Shoot Down His Plane," CBS News, April 9, 2025. www.cbsnews.com.
28. Quoted in Rachel Leingang, "Far-Right Conspiracies Abound After Second Apparent Trump Assassination Attempt," *The Guardian* (US edition), September 17, 2024. www.theguardian.com.
29. Quoted in Ali Abbas Ahmadi, "Ex-FBI Boss James Comey Investigated for Seashell Photo Seen as Threat to Trump," BBC, May 16, 2025. www.bbc.com.
30. Michael Van Beek, "N.Y. Report Shows Why Michigan's Top-Down COVID Response Went Wrong," Mackinac Center for Public Policy, June 28, 2024. www.mackinac.org.
31. Quoted in Ben Collins and Brandy Zadrozny, "In Trump's 'Liberate' Tweets, Extremists See a Call to Arms," NBC News, April 17, 2020. www.nbcnews.com.
32. Quoted in Emily Lawler, "'Words Matter' from Leaders like President Trump, Gov. Whitmer Says After Kidnapping Plot Revealed," MLive, October 9, 2020. www.mlive.com.
33. Quoted in Anti-Defamation League, "Proud Boys," January 16, 2025. www.adl.org.
34. John S. Hollywood, "On Reducing Public Fears and Threats of Political Violence," RAND Corporation, December 11, 2024. www.rand.org.

Chapter Five: Controlling the Spread of Misinformation

35. Quoted in Christopher Ingraham, "Misinformation Expert Cites Non-Existent Sources in Minnesota Deep Fake Case," Yahoo! News, November 20, 2024. www.yahoo.com.
36. Quoted in Christine Clark, "How AI Can Help Stop the Spread of Misinformation," UC San Diego Today, September 17, 2024. https://today.ucsd.edu.
37. Quoted in Agam Shah, "Google's AI Watermarks Will Identify Deepfakes," *Dark Reading*, May 15, 2024. www.darkreading.com.
38. Quoted in Aurélie Pugnet and Max Griera, "Von der Leyen Promises 'European Democracy Shield' to Combat Foreign Interference at EU Level," Euractiv, May 15, 2024. www.euractiv.com.
39. Quoted in Lindsey Kornick, "John Kerry Calls the First Amendment a 'Major Block' to Stopping 'Disinformation,'" Fox News, September 29, 2024. www.foxnews.com.
40. Quoted in Adam Satariano, "E.U. Prepares Major Penalties Against Elon Musk's X," *New York Times*, April 3, 2025. www.nytimes.com.
41. Quoted in Justin Hendrix, "Transcript: Mark Zuckerberg Announces Major Changes to Meta's Content Moderation Policies and Operations," Tech Policy Press, January 7, 2025. www.techpolicy.press.
42. Quoted in Max Zahn, "Here's Why Meta Ended Fact-Checking, According to Experts," ABC News, January 7, 2025. https://abcnews.go.com.
43. Quoted in James Taranto, "'Fact Checkers' Become Rent Seekers," *Wall Street Journal*, January 16, 2025. www.wsj.com.

FOR FURTHER RESEARCH

Books

Perry Carpenter, *FAIK: A Practical Guide to Living in a World of Deepfakes, Disinformation, and AI-Generated Deceptions*. Wiley, 2024.

Joanne Kenen et al., *Information Sick: How Journalism's Decline and Misinformation's Rise Are Harming Our Health—and What We Can Do About It*. Johns Hopkins University Press, 2025.

Barbara McQuade, *Attack from Within: How Disinformation Is Sabotaging America*. Seven Stories, 2024.

Cindy L. Otis, *True or False: A CIA Analyst's Guide to Spotting Fake News*. Square Fish, 2022.

Will Sommer, *Trust the Plan: The Rise of QAnon and the Conspiracy That Unhinged America*. Harper, 2023.

Paul Thagard, *Falsehoods Fly: Why Misinformation Spreads and How to Stop It*. Columbia University Press, 2024.

Internet Sources

Mike Isaac and Theodore Schleifer, "Meta Says It Will End Its Fact-Checking Program on Social Media Posts," *New York Times*, January 7, 2025. www.nytimes.com.

Sophia Melanson Ricciardone, "How AI Bots Spread Misinformation Online and Undermine Democratic Politics," *The Conversation*, July 24, 2024. https://theconversation.com.

H. Colleen Sinclair, "7 Steps to Disprove a Conspiracy Theory," *Scientific American*, May 14, 2024. www.scientificamerican.com.

Monica L. Wang, "POV: Health Misinformation Is Rampant on Social Media," *BU Today*, February 9, 2024. www.bu.edu.

Brandy Zadrozny, "Disinformation Poses an Unprecedented Threat in 2024—and the U.S. Is Less Ready than Ever," NBC News, January 18, 2024. www.nbcnews.com.

Organizations and Websites

American Medical Association (AMA)

www.ama-assn.org

The AMA is the largest national medical association in the United States. The AMA's mission is to promote public health. Its website contains articles such as "Social Media Networks Must Crack Down on Medical Misinformation" and "Combating Vaccine Misinformation Saves Lives."

Anti-Defamation League (ADL)

www.adl.org

The ADL is the leading global anti-hate organization. Founded in 1913, its timeless mission is stopping the defamation of the Jewish people and securing justice and fair treatment for all people. Its website includes a Glossary of Extremism and Hate and a list of Tools to Track Hate.

Center for American Progress (CAP)

www.americanprogress.org

The CAP is an independent, nonpartisan, public policy institute. The center believes an effective government can earn the trust of the American people. To build trust, the CAP searches for ways to fight disinformation and false stories on social media, as described in the article "Protecting Democracy Online in 2024 and Beyond."

Centers for Disease Control and Prevention (CDC)

www.cdc.gov

The CDC is the nation's leading science-based, data-driven, service organization that protects the public's health. To accomplish its mission, the CDC provides reliable health information that protects the United States against expensive and dangerous health threats. The CDC website contains articles about combating medical misinformation.

FactCheck.org

www.factcheck.org

FactCheck.org is a nonpartisan, nonprofit advocate for voters that aims to reduce the level of deception and confusion in US politics. It monitors the factual accuracy of what is said by major US political outlets. Its website includes a section called Debunking Viral Claims.

Hoover Institution

www.hoover.org

The Hoover Institution is a think tank devoted to the principles of individual, economic, and political freedom; private enterprise; and representative government. It seeks to secure and safeguard peace, improve the human condition, and limit government intrusion into individual lives. Its website features several analyses of AI and its effect on disinformation in elections.

RAND Corporation

www.rand.org

The RAND Corporation is a nonprofit, nonpartisan research organization that seeks to help improve policy and decision-making through research and analysis. It has promoted ways to detect conspiracy theories and other forms of disinformation on social media using machine learning and other tools.

INDEX

PICTURE CREDITS

Cover: kup/Shutterstock

6: lev radin/Shutterstock
9: John Cetrino/Polaris/Newscom
13: Michele Ursi/Shutterstock
17: Imago/Alamy
23: ZUMA Press, Inc./Alamy
25: Paul Christian Gordon/Alamy
29: Michael Brochstein/Sipa USA/Newscom
32: Associated Press
35: Ringo Chiu/Shutterstock
39: Associated Press
41: Peter Serocki/Shutterstock
45: Johnny Silvercloud/Shutterstock
47: Linaimages/Shutterstock
51: Fizkes/Shutterstock